# Keeping This World Safe

Written and
Illustrated by
Mary Hammond

# A BOOK by ME
## Hero Series

*History comes alive with true stories written by children for children*

A BOOK by ME is dedicated to the Quad Cities' Three Esthers

**Esther Avruch**    **Esther Katz**    **Esther Schiff**

Also, lovingly dedicated to Ida Kramer, Holocaust Historian, & Edith Levy, Jewish Holocaust Survivor & Author

**MISSION STATEMENT:**

A BOOK by ME® seeks to preserve the history of the Holocaust and other human rights issues. Our desire is to preserve the stories for the next generation so lessons of tolerance, empathy, hope and respect are not lost.

*Deb Bowen's work with young authors is important for our generation and the next. Without her, some stories may have gotten lost. Her work is geared towards realization and understanding, hence, prevention. I fully believe in the importance of her work for generations to come.*

Dr. Edith Rechter Levy, Ph.D
Holocaust Survivor, Author and Scholar

Dear Reader,

I'm from a small town in Illinois called Macomb. That's where the hero of our story, John Moon, lives, too. Western Illinois University is in our town, and the college is a big part of John's story. It was a big experience meeting John, writing his story and creating the artwork, too. It was a labor of love for a true American hero. Let me introduce you to John:

---

Name:       John Moon

Born:       April 3, 1916 in Macomb, Illinois

Family:     John's father, Frank, was a contractor and mother, Sarah, was a housewife. Much more than that, she was well known for helping people in need. There were many hobos who came through town from the railroad tracks. Sarah always had a kind word and a bite to eat for them. She became known as "Mother Moon." Frank and Sarah had ten children, five girls and five boys.

John Moon

Story:      After high school, John went to Western Illinois Teachers College (now called Western Illinois University) in Macomb. He graduated with a major in chemistry and got a good job at Caterpillar Inc. in Peoria. He was working there when he heard about the Japanese bombing Pearl Harbor. By this time he was married with one small child. Immediately, he knew he had to do his part to make the world a safer place for his little boy.

---

Sitting at the table with John and listening to him talk about Pearl Harbor and his reaction to the bombing being to protect his family, I was in awe. He made the history books I've read real to me. John said he was inspired by his college football coach, Colonel Ray Hanson, a WWI and WWII hero. Like Coach Hanson, John joined the Marines because he felt it was best to fight in small groups. Now 103 years old, John still believes the Marines are more mobile and the best.

He fought alongside his fellow Marines at Iwo Jima, one of the bloodiest battles in history. John says he is one of the luckiest men in the world. I think I was lucky to meet him and share his story with you.

Mary Hammond
Young Author

My name is John Moon. Do you want to hear my story? Where to start? Well, I was born on April 3, 1916. I am the youngest of ten kids. My dad, Frank Moon, was a contractor and builder, and my mother Sarah was a stay-at-home mom. Because my dad was a contractor and we had a garden and chickens, we did okay through the Great Depression, but we had our struggles just like everybody else.

    I was too young to remember, but my family likes to tell the story of when I got my arm stuck in mom's old ABC washing machine. I was about two when my mom put me on top of the washing machine. My sister had come back from school to pick up something, so my mom went to help her find it. In the meantime, I was on the washer messing around. I pushed down on the lever, which pulled my arm into the rollers. My arm was so stuck that someone from the hardware store had to come take the rollers apart to free my arm! I have a scar on my arm to this day.

I come from a musical family. Oh, how I remember the times when we would gather around the piano and sing as a family. One time my family made up the whole church choir! I love to sing! While I attended Western Illinois State Teachers College, now known as Western Illinois University, I sang in the glee club and sang a solo in a play. I graduated from Western in 1936 with a degree in chemistry, which helped me get a job at Caterpillar Tractor Company.

I married my wife Beatrice in 1936. When I heard about the attack on Pearl Harbor in 1941, I was working at Caterpillar testing steel samples before they were shipped off. I called my wife that day and said, "I think I should quit my job and enlist in the Marines to keep this world safe for our son Paul." I don't think she liked that very much, but I had to do it. So, I traveled to Chicago to enlist and there sat one of my friends from college!

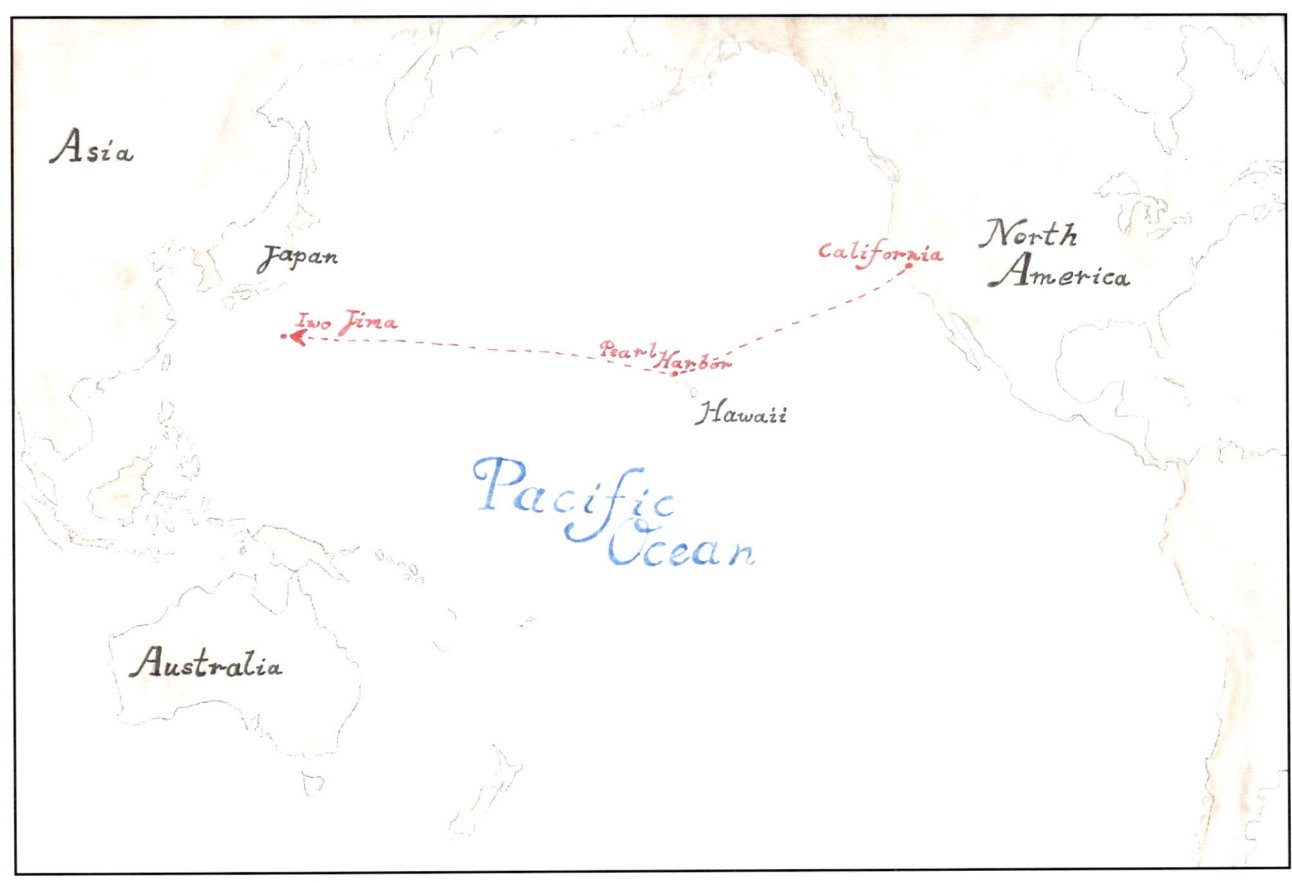

My basic training was at Camp Pendleton in California. My wife and son stayed there with me until I was shipped out. My rank was Private First Class (PFC) in the Marines. I was put on a ship with my fellow Marines. After we had made a stop at Pearl Harbor in Hawaii, we were on a boat to Iwo Jima for 40 days. Iwo Jima is an island 760 miles southeast of Japan. The United Sates wanted to capture Iwo Jima from Japan during World War II.

While I was away from home, I kept pictures of my wife, my son Paul, and my mother in my shirt pocket close to my heart. Arriving at Iwo Jima on February 19, 1945, we encountered heavy enemy fire. The gun fire was so bad that we could not stand and had to crawl most of the way to capture the third airfield. While crawling, our guns got clogged up with black sand from the island and would not work. It took us 13 days to get to the airfield.

To help keep our troops safe, one of our soldiers had the job of putting a marker out in front of the battle line whenever we advanced so our airplanes would know where not to fire. No one knew the soldier putting out the marker had been killed, so we advanced beyond the point where we were supposed to stop. Because the marker had not been moved, our own planes were firing on us. It was terrible! After 12 days in battle, our Sergeant and Corporal were killed. So, I had to assume the rank of Corporal. I led a three-man flamethrower team.

I am very proud to say that some of the soldiers in my Division raised the U.S. flag on Mount Suribachi, which gave all the Marines fighting on Iwo Jima hope of winning the battle. I was in the 5th Division, 2nd Battalion, Company E. While on the island, I saw terrible things. The battle of Iwo Jima resulted in 6,800 deaths of U.S military men. I am very lucky to be alive.

I was shot in the back of my leg, which probably saved my life, because I was transported off the island to Pearl Harbor so I could recover. I was awarded a Purple Heart medal. Everyone who shed blood received a Purple Heart. After my military service, I was reunited with my family, and we settled back down in Macomb, Illinois where I had grown up.

Beatrice and I had three kids: Paul, David, and Jeanine. I worked several jobs after the war. I was a carpenter, I ran a café, and I even taught driver's education at the Macomb High School, just to name a few. I still love to sing! I sang the National Anthem at a girl's basketball game at Western Illinois University when I was 100 years old.

# From the Family Album

John Moon parents and family

Beatrice Moon,
John's wife

John's oldest son Paul
in a little Marine outfit

At the age of 101, accompanied by his son,
David, and daughter, Jeanine, John participated
in The Greater Peoria Honor Flight. He was
recognized as the oldest veteran to have flown.

John at the United States Marine
Corps War Memorial (Iwo Jima
Memorial)

Deb Bowen, Creator of A BOOK by ME, Hero
John Moon, Sharon Taylor A BOOK by ME Story
Coordinator and young author Mary Hammond

# John Moon

## U.S. Marines, WWII

There were ten children growing up in Macomb, Illinois in John Moon's family. John had five sisters and four brothers. They were a musical family, and all sang in the church choir. His parents were affected during the Great Depression, but they had a garden and some chickens in the back yard so food was always available for their family.

After high school, John went to college and majored in chemistry. He met the love of his life, a woman named Beatrice (Bee) from London Mills, a small town about 40 miles away. While they were courting, he had the idea of taking her a dozen red roses, but it was very cold outside and he was riding on his motorcycle. He tried to keep them warm, but by the time he got to Bee's house, they had frozen and turned black. His efforts were appreciated and he was thanked with a kiss. They were married in 1936 and soon had a son named Paul.

John was working at Caterpillar, Inc. when he heard about Pearl Harbor in December 1941. He decided to join the Marines and went home to tell Beatrice of his plans. Off he went to the recruiting station in Chicago with a teammate from his football days in college. He was given a physical exam and enlisted in the Marines, inspired by his college football coach, Ray Hanson.

John went to boot camp at Camp Pendleton in California and later on to Hawaii to finish his training. Then John and his fellow Marines were put on a ship, and after making a stop at Pearl Harbor, they sailed into the Pacific Ocean and stayed there for the next 40 days. They were not allowed to get off the ship and had no idea where they were going. One day, the officers in charge handed out a map of an island and informed them they would be going to Iwo Jima. Like the others, John wondered, "Where is Iwo Jima?"

He learned it's located about 760 miles southeast of Japan. The Allies wanted to capture the island from Japan as a strategic move because of three airfields located there. The 5th Marine Division was told to get their gear on because "we are going in now." The men scrambled to get everything ready to take off and got aboard a Higgins boat headed to the island. These boats carry approximately 36 men and are long and rectangular. The front of the boat has a large door designed to open once the boat hits land.

But, when John's boat got there, the enemy's fire damaged the front end of the boat and the ramp jammed up so it could not lower down. They were forced to climb over the edge of the boat and drop into the water with 80 pounds of gear on their backs. They scrambled for the beach with the enemy's bullets flying all around them. If you stood up, you got shot, so John and the other marines crawled in the sand. They crawled all the way to the west side of the island to capture the third and unfinished airfield.

When you are crawling on the ground, your weapon is also on the ground, and it gets full of sand. John could not keep his Browning automatic rifle unclogged. It would not fire a single shot the entire time he was on the island. All he had was his 11-inch KA-BAR knife, which he still has today. It didn't give John a lot of comfort knowing he only had a knife to defend himself.

His unit traveled for thirteen days to the airfield, crawling most of the way. In addition to his weapons, John had two photos in his shirt pocket next to his heart. One was of his mother and the other of wife Beatrice and son, Paul.

The weather was nice while on the island, with a little sprinkle of rain each day. The journey to the airfields was treacherous, with the marines always trying to avoid the enemy's bullets. It was challenging, because the Japanese were dug in pretty deep and had tunnels and caves all up and down the island. The marines used flame throwers to draw them out.

John and his fellow Marines would use what they could for cover. They often used shell holes, a cavity in the ground made by an explosion, for protection. Sometimes the enemy beat them to the hole, since they used them, too. The Japanese set traps in many of these shell holes. One day, John dropped in one hole and realized his hand was inches away from a trap. If he had hit it, it would have exploded. He felt he was lucky.

When the men needed rest, they would partner up. One would keep watch while the other rested in a foxhole, a small pit the men would dig to use for cover. John didn't feel like they slept much, but at least they rested. Just as the Marines made it to the airfield, John felt a sharp jab of pain. He grabbed his inner left thigh and saw blood. He was shot. They enemy's bullet took a chunk of flesh out about as big as his little finger. Again, he felt lucky that his wound wasn't serious and he could still walk. John tried to warn his buddy "Muncie" not to come toward him, but he came anyway and was hit in the groin. His wound was worse and needed immediate medical treatment. John wrapped up his leg with his army pack, slung his friend's arm over his shoulder, and the two hobbled to the company aid station on the beach.

John felt sure the enemy would shoot at them. "But, believe it or not, we were not fired upon. Not one time, as we were walking back," John Says. "If they saw us, maybe they thought we were through and didn't waste ammunition on us. I lucked out. I've been lucky all my life."

The two men were taken to the hospital ship. Because of his wound, John got off that island after thirteen days. He firmly believes if he hadn't been shot, he wouldn't have gotten off the island alive. John was awarded a Purple Heart and settled back to life in his hometown of Macomb where he and his wife had two more children, David and Jeanine. He worked at several jobs over the years: he was a carpenter, ran a cafe, worked at an Andes Candies store and an insurance company, taught driver's education, and worked security at Wesley Village (a retirement home) well into his 90s.

Today, at 103, John says, "I feel like I'm one of the luckiest men in the world, and I have been lucky all my life. Thirteen is my lucky number. Those thirteen days ... that was a heck of a life."

*"War is a grim, cruel business, a business justified only as a means of sustaining the forces of good against those of evil."*
**-General Dwight D. Eisenhower**

## About the Author/Illustrator
### Mary Hammond

I live in central Illinois amongst the corn fields. I am 15 years old. My mom home schools me along with my three other siblings. Among other things, I enjoy baking, sewing, painting, pottery and drawing. I like to write fun little stories and read true stories during the World War II time period. I enjoyed retelling Mr. Moon's story. I loved getting to know him during our interview. He had such an awesome personality. I think it's so important to keep these veterans' stories alive.

*"It was such an honor to meet living history. Hearing John's story gave me a greater appreciation for the sacrifices our soldiers made. It's easy to forget that these men were regular people just like us, who wanted to protect the future of our country. Hearing John's story helped me to see that."*
**-Mary Hammond**

John Moon and his young
author Mary Hammond

# LEARNING STATION

## Vocabulary and Key Terms

**airfield –** an area of land set aside for aircraft to take off and land

**anthem –** a patriotic song adopted by a country as an expression of national identity

**basic training –** initial training of physical activity and behavior discipline for military personnel

**corporal –** a noncommissioned army officer rank between private and sergeant

**enlist –** to be enrolled in the armed forces

**flamethrower –** a weapon that sprays out burning fuel

**glee club –** a musical or choir group that sing short songs called glees

**Great Depression –**the economic crisis or period of slow business in the United States and other countries, beginning with the stock-market crash in October 1929 and continuing through most of the 1930's

**Marines –** a branch of the armed forces that serve both on land and at sea

**Pearl Harbor –**American naval station in Hawaii attacked without warning by the Japanese on December 7, 1941, leading to the United States entering World War II

**Purple Heart –** a United States military medal awarded to those wounded or killed in battle

## Short Summary

John Moon was born in Macomb, Illinois in 1916. After high school, he studied at Western Illinois Teachers College and graduated with a major in Chemistry. While working at Caterpillar Inc., he heard about the Japanese attack on Pearl Harbor. He told his wife he wanted to enlist in the Marines. After basic training, he was sent by ship to Iwo Jima in the Pacific. He fought for 13 days trying to take over an airfield from the Japanese. John was shot and received a Purple Heart for his bravery in combat.

## MLA Citation

Hammond, Mary. *Keeping This World Safe.* Vol. 37. Monmouth, IL: Never Forget, 2021. Print. Hero Ser.

## Topics Covered

Bravery
Honor
Patriotism
Service
World War II

# LEARNING STATION

## Thinking Strategies

- Making Connections – Connect the reading to the existing schema.
- Questioning – Question before, during, and after reading. Consider the content, ideas, and events.
- Visualizing – Use background knowledge, make mental pictures of the text.
- Inferring – Use knowledge to infer the underlying theme or idea to interpret meaning.
- Determining Importance – Develop summarizing skills.
- Synthesizing – Make sense of important information to construct deeper meaning.

## Pre-Reading Activity

Iwo Jima is one of the Japanese Volcano islands 760 miles southeast off the coast of Japan. In Japan the island is known as Iwo To. It became a major battle site during World War II. On February 19, 1945, Americans invaded the island and fought for five weeks to take over the island. Clint Eastwood directed two movies about the battle: *Flags of Our Fathers* about the battle from the American perspective and *Letters from Iwo Jima* from the Japanese perspective. View the films to learn about these two perspectives.

## Related Literature & Media

A BOOK by ME Hero Series*
- Book#7 *Pearl Harbor Classified* is about Dean Urick, who survived the West Loch Disaster at Pearl Harbor.
- Book#22 *A Day Never Forgotten* is about Navy Veteran Eldon Baxter and his accounts of the attack on Pearl Harbor.
- Book#24 *Moonlight Serenade* is about Elsie Bossola Little, a woman who joined the U.S. Marines during WWII.

Other Resources*
- *Unknown Valor* by Martha MacCallum is the story from Pearl Harbor to Iwo Jima, piecing together stories from letters and recollections.
- *The Things Our Fathers Saw* by Matthew A. Rozell is a collection of true stories from U.S. solders about the Pacific Theater.
- *You are There! Pearl Harbor, December 7, 1941* by Dona Herweck Rice is a Time for Kids Nonfiction Reader about Pearl Harbor.

*Preview all literature for appropriateness for your classroom

## Technology

Have students write mini-book reports to post on the A BOOK by ME Facebook page where others will read about their opinion of the story. Review with students how to write descriptions and to summarize. Include the theme and lessons learned. Remind students to be respectful in their writings. All posts on the Facebook page will be monitored.

 facebook.com / A BOOK by ME

# LEARNING STATION

## Discussion Questions

1) John grew up with five sisters and four brothers. They all sang in church choir and helped in the garden together. What would be the benefits of having a big family like John's? What were the struggles for a big family during the Great Depression?

2) When John heard about the attack on Pearl Harbor in December 1941, he decided he wanted to join the Marines. His wife, Beatrice, wasn't fond of the idea. Why do you think John wanted to enlist? What do you think Beatrice's hesitations might have been?

3) After basic training at Camp Pendleton in California, John and his fellow Marines boarded a ship for 40 days on the way to Iwo Jima. What do you think it would be like to be on a ship for 40 days? What problems could arise from that situation?

4) John spent 13 days in Iwo Jima. His gun was clogged from sand, so he couldn't shoot. He had to swim while being shot at, almost set off a trap in a hole, and was shot in the thigh. The Japanese had tunnels all over the island in which to hide. How do you think John felt on the island? In which ways would you have to rely on your fellow Marines?

## Extended Activities

A) John comes from a musical family. He remembers gathering around the piano to sing. Create a song or lyrical poem about John's life. Perform the song or poem.

B) The attack on Pearl Harbor was a pivotal part of John's story. It motivated him to enlist in the Marines. View the original news broadcasts of the attack online. Imagine being John in 1941. Write a paragraph about how the broadcasts make you feel and the decision to enlist as John did.

C) Find Iwo Jima on a map or globe. Draw the island and locate the three airfields. Next to your drawing, add photographs of Iwo Jima, and also include animals and plants that are on the island. Record facts about the island, such as, the climate, history, and information about Mount Suribachi. When the research is complete, present the project.

D) The U.S. Marine Corps dedicated the Marine Corps War Memorial near the Arlington Cemetery in Virginia in 1954. The memorial is also known as the Iwo Jima Memorial. The memorial statue depicts the famous photograph taken by Joe Rosenthal of six Marines raising the U.S. flag at Iwo Jima on February 23, 1945. The statue was created by sculptor Felix W. de Weldon. Illustrate the iconic picture and write your thoughts on the bravery of the Marines that fought in Iwo Jima.

# LEARNING STATION

## Bullying Definition

According to Olweus Bullying Prevention Program: "A person is bullied when he or she is exposed, repeatedly and over time, to negative actions on the part of one or more other persons, and he or she has difficulty defending himself or herself."

## Discussion Questions Relating to Bullying

Do you see an example of bullying in *Keeping This World Safe?*
How does this story compare to bullying situations in your own school and community?
What can you do to stop bullying from taking place?

## Bullying Role Playing

Role playing is a way for students to internalize different responses and practices to reduce conflict in social situations. Review the possible coping strategies with students. Discuss how to deal with a specific bullying situation. Once the group decides on an appropriate coping strategy(s), students can act it out. Take note that the bully could react in a variety of different ways.

4 ways to describe emotion:

- controlled
- hated
- manipulated
- unsafe

Situation: A boy logs onto his social media and sees threatening messages from strangers. He doesn't tell anyone about these messages because he doesn't know who is sending them. What could the boy do?

## Bullying Coping Strategies

- **Avoidance** – Try to find a way to ignore the bully. Sometimes attention is what the bully wants.
- **Assertiveness** – Sometimes the best way to deal with a bully is to defend yourself by telling them to leave you alone. If you are watching someone else being bullied, stand up for that person.
- **Friendship** – Strength in numbers will sometimes put a bully in his/her place. Find someone who will stand up with you. Be the person who defends a victim of a bully.
- **Education** – Find an adult (teacher, parent, mentor, etc.) to help you educate others about treating all people with respect. If a bully won't back down, get someone with authority to help you stop the situation.

## Advice from John's Story

Fight for what you believe.
Have students discuss and/or write how this advice could be used in their life.

# LEARNING STATION

## Comprehension Questions
Cite evidence from the story text in your answers.

1. How did John's family survive the Great Depression? _____
_____
_____
_____

2. How did John's arm get stuck in the washing machine? _____
_____
_____

3. Why was music important to John? _____
_____
_____
_____

4. What important decision did John make because of the attack on Pearl Harbor? _____
_____
_____
_____

5. How did Beatrice react to John's decision? _____
_____
_____

6. What was fighting in the Iwo Jima battle like for John? _____
_____
_____

7. Why was John awarded the Purple Heart medal? _____
_____
_____

8. What did you learn from John's story? _____
_____
_____

# LEARNING STATION

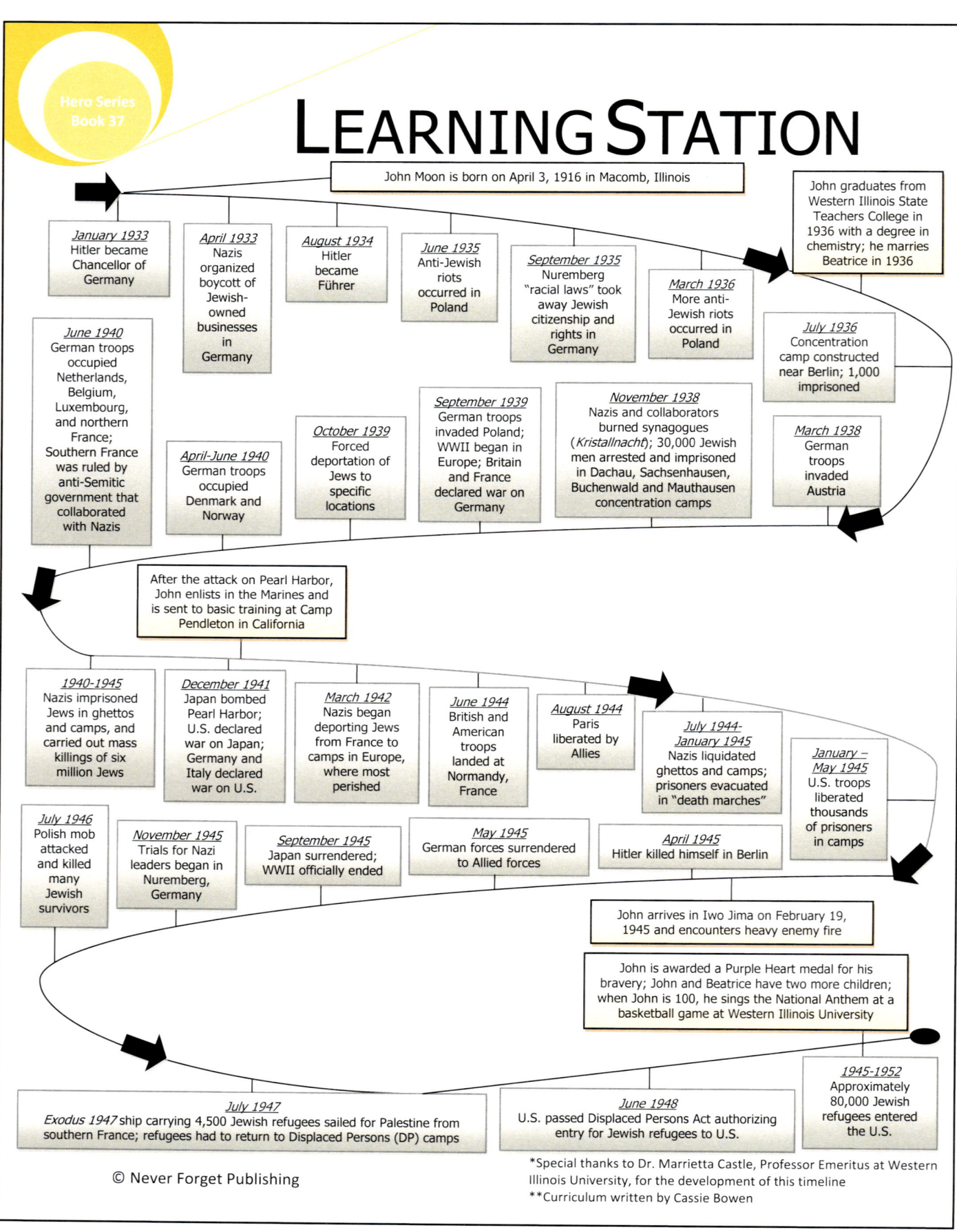

John Moon is born on April 3, 1916 in Macomb, Illinois

*January 1933* Hitler became Chancellor of Germany

*April 1933* Nazis organized boycott of Jewish-owned businesses in Germany

*August 1934* Hitler became Führer

*June 1935* Anti-Jewish riots occurred in Poland

*September 1935* Nuremberg "racial laws" took away Jewish citizenship and rights in Germany

*March 1936* More anti-Jewish riots occurred in Poland

John graduates from Western Illinois State Teachers College in 1936 with a degree in chemistry; he marries Beatrice in 1936

*July 1936* Concentration camp constructed near Berlin; 1,000 imprisoned

*June 1940* German troops occupied Netherlands, Belgium, Luxembourg, and northern France; Southern France was ruled by anti-Semitic government that collaborated with Nazis

*April-June 1940* German troops occupied Denmark and Norway

*October 1939* Forced deportation of Jews to specific locations

*September 1939* German troops invaded Poland; WWII began in Europe; Britain and France declared war on Germany

*November 1938* Nazis and collaborators burned synagogues (*Kristallnacht*); 30,000 Jewish men arrested and imprisoned in Dachau, Sachsenhausen, Buchenwald and Mauthausen concentration camps

*March 1938* German troops invaded Austria

After the attack on Pearl Harbor, John enlists in the Marines and is sent to basic training at Camp Pendleton in California

*1940-1945* Nazis imprisoned Jews in ghettos and camps, and carried out mass killings of six million Jews

*December 1941* Japan bombed Pearl Harbor; U.S. declared war on Japan; Germany and Italy declared war on U.S.

*March 1942* Nazis began deporting Jews from France to camps in Europe, where most perished

*June 1944* British and American troops landed at Normandy, France

*August 1944* Paris liberated by Allies

*July 1944-January 1945* Nazis liquidated ghettos and camps; prisoners evacuated in "death marches"

*January – May 1945* U.S. troops liberated thousands of prisoners in camps

*July 1946* Polish mob attacked and killed many Jewish survivors

*November 1945* Trials for Nazi leaders began in Nuremberg, Germany

*September 1945* Japan surrendered; WWII officially ended

*May 1945* German forces surrendered to Allied forces

*April 1945* Hitler killed himself in Berlin

John arrives in Iwo Jima on February 19, 1945 and encounters heavy enemy fire

John is awarded a Purple Heart medal for his bravery; John and Beatrice have two more children; when John is 100, he sings the National Anthem at a basketball game at Western Illinois University

*July 1947* *Exodus 1947* ship carrying 4,500 Jewish refugees sailed for Palestine from southern France; refugees had to return to Displaced Persons (DP) camps

*June 1948* U.S. passed Displaced Persons Act authorizing entry for Jewish refugees to U.S.

*1945-1952* Approximately 80,000 Jewish refugees entered the U.S.

*Special thanks to Dr. Marrietta Castle, Professor Emeritus at Western Illinois University, for the development of this timeline
**Curriculum written by Cassie Bowen

# A BOOK by ME®
## OPERATION WRITE NOW

**"I'm asking ordinary children to do something extraordinary!"**

**Deb Bowen, Creator & Director**
www.abookbyme.com

I'm asking ordinary children all over the world to use their talents to share extraordinary stories. Many students write about Holocaust survivors, Righteous Gentiles (non-Jews who risked their lives to save the Jewish people), prison camp liberators and other important stories of World War II. Since this generation is getting older, the time to interview them, write and illustrate their important story is RIGHT NOW!

Some students are deciding to tell important stories about human rights or heroes as well. Check out the website and then decide what interests you. The writer's guidelines are online, and you can register your story once you decide who your subject will be. Also, online you will find a sample of a newspaper article you could use to find a subject in your hometown. Talking to a grandparent, visiting nursing homes, VFW or meeting with a local historian might lead you to a possible story.

All authors / illustrators must be age 18 or under to qualify. All submissions will be given consideration for the A BOOK by ME® series, but there is no guarantee the work will be published.

It is my hope you have learned from the book you just read and are interested in reading more work by young authors. It would delight me to know you are inspired to write a book about a subject important to you.

*Be careful and watch yourselves closely so you do not forget the things your eyes have seen or let them slip from your heart as long as you live. Teach them to your children and to your children's children.*
**Deuteronomy 4:9**

# love like lorraine
## purses with purpose

Love Like Lorraine was created to honor my beautiful mother. Lorraine was a simple farm wife with eight kids, but always found it in her heart to give. As a kid, I was amazed to see her give money I knew she really couldn't spare. She lived through the Great Depression and she knew what it was like to go through hard times. To honor her memory, I'm challenging women:

**1** clean old purses or drawstring bags you have at home

**2** fill them with things people can always use, such as: kleenex, Tylenol, a billfold, brush, make up, feminine items, wet wipes, warm socks, gloves, a scarf, deck of cards, gift card for coffee, etc.

**3** donate to a homeless shelter, women's shelter, crisis center, prison ministries, refugee organizations, schools etc.

**4** encourage your youth organization to collect and fill purses

It's exciting to think that these love bags will be given to someone in need! What a blessing! I encourage you to gather together with friends for lunch or a house party asking them to bring a bag or two filled up ready to donate. It can be a casual and fun meeting. We can all love like Lorraine.

Deb Bowen
abookbyme@gmail.com

like us on facebook and share your experience!

22